The
ART of
LISTENING
in a HEALING
WAY

The
ART of
LISTENING
in a HEALING
WAY

Text and Photography by
James E. Miller

WILL⊗WGREEN®
PUBLISHING

To Susan,
so wise, so generous, so loving.

To Jinnie,
so astute, so gracious, so caring.

Copyright 2003
by James E. Miller

WILLQWGREEN®
P U B L I S H I N G

10351 Dawson's Creek Boulevard, Suite B
Fort Wayne, Indiana 46825
260/490-2222

Library of Congress Control Number
2003096247

ISBN 1-885933-35-5

The most agreeable of all companions
is a simple, frank person,
without any high pretensions
to an oppressive greatness;
one who loves life,
and understands the use of it;
obliging, alike, at all hours;
above all, of a golden temper,
and steadfast as an anchor.
For such a one we gladly exchange
the greatest genius, the most brilliant wit,
the profoundest thinker.

G. E. Lessing

Table of Contents

Foreword

When was the first time you felt really listened to?

Who did the listening?

What did you speak about?

How did you feel as the experience unfolded, and afterward?

Why do you think this experience stays with you through all the years?

The first time I remember feeling really listened to I was sixteen years old. I had driven by myself in the family car to a doctor's office in Indianapolis, fifty miles away. A physician in my hometown recommended that I see a skin specialist for my adolescent acne.

The reception area was crowded when I arrived and I expected a long wait. But I was soon ushered to the exam room, and not long after, the doctor entered. He performed a routine examination of my face, neck, and chest as he asked questions about my condition. How long had I had it? What made it worse? What had I done for it? How much did it bother me?

As I put on my shirt, he pulled up a chair and began asking a different line of questions. He wanted to know not about my condition but about me. Did I like school? What parts of it? Did I have friends? Hobbies? What was I good at? He asked about my family, my place in the family, and my relationship with my parents. He wondered if I was experiencing any difficulties. He wanted to know about my feelings.

This well-spoken, learned man seemed interested in everything I said. He smiled, nodded, occasionally made notes. He gave me plenty of time to answer his questions. "All those other people are waiting to see this man," I remember thinking to myself, "yet he acts as if he has all the time in the world for me, and as if what I am saying is worthwhile."

How long did he spend with me? Maybe twenty or twenty-five minutes. It seemed like an amazingly long time for a busy specialist to spend listening to a self-conscious adolescent who lived a pretty boring life. I remember that as I left his office that afternoon, I felt that I mattered somehow, and so did my thoughts and feelings, including those I shared with hardly anyone. Forty years later I can still recall how good it felt to be listened to in such an intentional way.

I'd like to think that for at least a few times in my life since then, I've been as good a listener as that doctor. I'd like to think that, as a result, some other people have felt as if they mattered too. I'd like to think the same is true of all of us.

Even so, I'm aware that sometimes I haven't listened nearly as well as I was listened to that day. I've caught myself daydreaming instead of paying attention. I've thoughtlessly interrupted the other person to insert my own thoughts. I've concentrated on what I was preparing to say rather than on what the other person was carefully saying. Perhaps you've done the same. If that's the case, I invite you to look over my shoulder as I write this book for myself. Maybe there's something in it for you too.

Introduction

There is a significant difference between hearing and listening.

Hearing is the natural functioning of the human auditory system. This includes the ear, its connections to the nervous system, and those parts of the brain that process sound. Hearing has to do with human physiology.

Listening, on the other hand, starts with the effortless functioning of that auditory system and stretches it into new dimensions.

Listening involves, first of all, choosing to pay close attention to the various sounds that come our way. It is a conscious choice. We might do this by opening our awareness to the whole host of sounds floating around us at a given moment. Or we might concentrate on a specific sound, isolating, for example, a bird's song from all the surrounding noises while we're standing on a sidewalk. Yet in addition to receiving and attending to sound, listening also involves assigning meaning to what is heard. "That bird's song seems cheerful; it brightens my day."

Hearing is something that happens to us. Listening is something in which we choose to participate.

Most of us learn to be listeners quite early in life. It's an important way in which we get to know the world. As we learn to listen, we gather the meaning of words and the structure of language, enabling us to think, speak, and expand our knowledge in many directions.

Listening is the primary mode of most formal education. Estimates are that between 45% and 75% of one's time in school is spent listening. As we grow into adulthood, we commonly spend large portions of our days in the practice of listening, as a part of our work, our family life, our social activities, and our leisure pursuits.

Interestingly, for all its importance in life, listening is not generally taught as a subject. It's estimated there are 50,000 speech courses in U. S. colleges every year. But how many courses are there in listening? Only a handful. Book titles in print related to speaking number several thousand, while titles related to listening amount to a few hundred.

Somehow we assume we were all born good listeners. Consequently, there is not much to compel us to learn how to listen better. Having read this far, you're bucking the trend.

Not all listening is alike. Different life encounters call for different ways of listening.

Much of the time we *listen casually*. We're paying attention to sounds and voices without really concentrating on them. At any moment we can choose to listen more intently or specifically, but short of a reason to do so, our attention is cursory and unfocused.

Sometimes *we listen for comprehension*. There are facts we're expected to learn, ideas we want to understand, or situations about which we wish to become clearer. The goal here is to grasp information and retain it.

There are occasions when *we listen critically*. We attune ourselves not so much in order to know but to make a judgment. Do I agree or disagree? Does this argument persuade me or not? Often a decision is at stake. Shall I vote yes or no? Shall I give my assent to what is being asked of me? The facts themselves may be elusive, contradictory, or even nonexistent. So we listen for more—inconsistencies in the reasoning, inflections in the voice.

At other times *we listen appreciatively*. We savor sounds that give us pleasure or touch us at a deeper level. This can happen as we tune in to a favorite song, inspirational music, or sounds from nature. We attend appreciatively to cantatas, poetry readings, and the telling of a well-crafted story.

At times *we listen therapeutically*. We commonly associate counselors, psychiatrists, clergy, and other trained professionals with this kind of listening, although it can also be done by individuals without formal training. The meaning of the Greek word from which *therapeutic* is derived defines this experience: "to nurse, serve, or cure." When we listen therapeutically, we have a goal in mind—to help the one who is speaking. We call upon our insights, experiences, and abilities as well as our sense of caring to serve the other person in hope that she or he is made better or cured.

There is a sixth kind of listening—*healing listening*. While it shares some of the same characteristics as therapeutic listening, the differences are distinct.

Healing listening has to do with being rather than with doing. We listen not to help someone but simply to be with someone, to stay with them for a while, perhaps to approach understanding them. We listen not so that we can offer our insight or advice to another but so that wisdom can be explored and insight revealed through that person's words, thoughts, and feelings. Or not. Wisdom doesn't have to come. Nor insight. Perhaps the other person will experience a sense of relief or release. They may feel less burdened or more assured, less isolated or more validated. They may feel somehow challenged or invited through this experience. Perhaps they'll come away feeling more awakened.

Healing listening favors wholeness. That's what the root word for *heal* means: "to become hale, to make whole." When we listen to others in a healing way, we affirm the belief that they can become more complete as they express and claim what they have within them to say. This increasing completeness usually occurs gradually, progressively, but sometimes it happens quite quickly. At times the other person is aware of this growing wholeness while they're speaking or as they finish; at other times they become aware only upon reflection. They may have words to define what's happening to them, or the experience may rest beyond their ability to describe or understand it.

When we listen in a healing way, we carry no agenda for the other person or for ourselves. We listen because we choose to listen, without knowing what will transpire, without needing to know. We listen because the other person is worth being listened to, however little or much we know about them, however much we're alike or unalike. We listen because listening can put us in touch with life and with all that life both promises and delivers.

We listen because we know from our own experience how gently affirming it is when someone carefully hears us in a way that honors who we are as whole human beings. We listen because we know how freeing it is to be accepted just as we are, without preconceptions and without judgment.

Because healing listening is about being rather than about doing, it cannot be exactly prescribed or programmed. Different people will respond in different ways. What suits one situation may not suit another. Adhering carefully to a given set of rules will not guarantee that one is being a healing listener, or even listening at all. Rigid adherence to a method, in fact, can block such listening.

At the same time, some guidelines can be helpful, and some general rules do hold for many situations. We'll name a few of these principles in the following pages. Some will pertain to your particular situation more than others. Use the ones that apply and let fall away those that don't. You'll know which are which.

The ear is the way.
The Upanishads

~

The ears are two music-rooms.
Thomas Dekker

~

The eyes believe themselves.
The ears believe other people.
German Proverb

Healing listening is founded on wonder.

Hearing is a sense most of us take for granted. It seems so simple. The simple act of hearing another person's words, however, is an astonishing process.

Those spoken syllables travel to you as air waves, striking first your flexible eardrum, making it vibrate, which in turn shakes a tiny bone, the malleus, which jostles a second bone, the incus, which in turn wiggles a third, the stapes. The lever action of these three bones intensifies the effect of the original air wave so it can move through another, denser medium—liquid.

The stapes jiggles the base of the cochlea, a pea-sized, liquid-filled, coiled tube, sending waves down its entire length. These fluctuations wash over four rows of 16,000 microscopic hair cells, causing them to quiver in various ways. To produce the highest frequencies, some of these hair cells must respond as quickly as 20,000 times a second. Each quiver of each cell sends a message to the cochlea's center where the organ of Corti converts these vibrations into neural energy. Traveling now through nerves, these messages about each individual sound are hurried to the brain, where, after several relays, they end up at various sites in the cerebral cortex. There all these nerve charges are instantaneously processed, and as they come together, they are interpreted. When that happens, we "hear" a sound, a syllable, a word.

This common auditory contrivance is nothing less than amazing. Processing sound 1,000 times faster than the eye can process light, it is puzzling in its complexity. It is astounding in its sophistication. And it is nothing less than wondrous in its execution.

Healing listening rests on that wonder and never ventures far away.

Listening looks easy, but it is not simple.
Every head is a world.
Cuban Proverb

The most difficult thing of all,
to keep quiet and listen.
Aulus Gellius

If to talk to oneself when alone is folly,
it must be doubly unwise to listen to oneself
in the presence of others.
Baltasar Gracian

Healing listening begins with a triple intention.

Your listening does not happen magically. It occurs only with focus. The first focus that's asked of you is a decision that is, in reality, three separate decisions.

The most basic question is, "Will I do more than merely hear? Will I listen?" When you listen, you commit yourself. You prepare to get involved, to invest energy in what's awaiting you. Your listening may be a quiet labor of love, but can still be labor.

The second question is an extension of the first: "Will I listen to this person, in this place, at this moment?" This person may be easy to be with, or difficult. The environment may feel comfortable, or it may seem distracting. The timing may be convenient, or it may be just the opposite. You may feel open and ready, or you may not.

If the situation is not ideal (and so many times it's not), what will you do? Decline to listen? Suggest an alternative? Proceed as best you can? Healing listening asks you to say "yes" at some level to a particular time, place, and person. Of course, no one may hear this "yes" but you.

The third intention regards your purpose: "Will I listen with the other person's needs foremost in mind?" Listening in a healing way means being clear about your desire to support the other person's increasing wholeness. While your listening does not cause that wholeness, it can be an avenue for it.

Most likely you'll answer these questions quickly, if not instantaneously. You may answer them subconsciously. Yet answer them you must. For by naming fully your intentions, if only to yourself, you can then bring to this experience your full resolve and energy. As a healing listener you'll need both.

You listen to so much more than I can say.
You hear consciousness. You go with me
where the words I say can't carry you.
Kahlil Gibran

Oh, the comfort, the inexpressible comfort
of feeling safe with a person;
having neither to weigh thoughts
nor to measure words but to pour them all out,
just as it is, chaff and grain together,
knowing that a faithful hand will take and sift them,
keeping what is worth keeping, and then,
with the breath of kindness, blow the rest away.
Mary Ann Evans

Healing listening stays true to the purpose of listening.

When people open to you, you may feel drawn into their lives. As you become aware of what's happening to them and what they're dealing with, you may wish to do what you can to help. It can be satisfying to be able to assist others, to know you have made a significant difference.

So depending on the situation and what you sense needs to be addressed, you may be tempted to help fix what's obviously wrong or do what seems naturally right. You may try to help others feel better and be happier. You may wish to lead them to new insight, fresh meaning, or clear hope. Those all seem like valid goals. When you serve as a healing listener, however, your purpose is not to do any of these things. Your purpose is not to help—it is to listen.

To listen in a healing way is to *listen carefully*, paying real attention to all that's being said and not said. You *listen respectfully*, holding both the other person and whatever they have to say with clear regard. You *listen caringly*, allowing a warmth to develop between you if it feels natural, always desiring what is best for the other. You *listen compassionately*, accepting the one you're with just as they are, without comparing them to others or to yourself. And you *listen believingly*, trusting in the healing potential of those who verbally and nonverbally share their lives with you.

As you stay true to your purpose of remaining a listener, healing and wholeness are ultimately more likely to occur than if you scurried about, doing everything you could to be helpful.

Go to your bosom;
Knock there;
and ask your heart,
what it doth know.
William Shakespeare

No one who has not a complete knowledge of self
will ever have a true understanding of another.
Friedrich von Hardenberg

Tend to yourself and it is enough.
Joseph of Optima

A healing listener listens to self before listening to another.

Before making yourself available to someone who wishes to speak, you owe it to both of you to know something about this self of yours that you're making available. What is going on with you these days in general and this day in particular? Are you happy, or sad, or hovering somewhere in between? Are you anxious? Fearful? Excited? Harried? Bored? You may be carrying over feelings from a disturbing encounter earlier in the day. A pressing problem may be doing just that—pressing on you.

Be aware of how you're bringing yourself to the time just ahead. Do you feel ready to listen? Do you really want to listen? Are you comfortable listening? What are your feelings about this person before you? What are your feelings about yourself right now?

By probing in this way, you clarify what is yours, and only yours, to deal with. Then it's less likely that you'll inadvertently confuse your issues with the other person's, or that you'll project your feelings onto them. Your priority is to be honest with yourself: "This is who I am today and what I feel right now." Just as you strive to listen compassionately to other people, you strive no less for yourself.

You can do one thing more: you can choose to place your personal feelings to one side for the time being, whether that time is counted in minutes or hours. This does not mean you deny or forget whatever is stirring within you or swirling around you. It simply means you're clearing a space inside so you are sufficiently open to receiving what the other person has to offer.

Listening first to yourself is a thoughtful way to begin listening to another.

Hospitality consists in a little fire,
a little food, and an immense quiet.
Ralph Waldo Emerson

No one is so rich
that he does not need another's help;
no one so poor as not to be useful
in some way to his fellow man;
and the disposition to ask assistance
from others with confidence,
and to grant it with kindness,
is part of our very nature.
Pope Leo XIII

Healing listening involves an equal relationship that is lived out in an unequal way.

There is nothing about being a listener that elevates you. Whatever the other person's portion of disappointment or heartache, you may know a similar share. Whatever sense of loss they have experienced, you may also experience. Whatever their shortcomings or failings, you are not immune to falling short and falling down yourself. Both of you are, in every way, equally human.

You are, in addition, equally partnered. The act of listening is no more important than that of speaking. The one who listens and the one who is listened to depend upon one another in the same measure.

You are equally capable. There is nothing inherent in your role as listener that makes you any smarter, wiser, or better than your counterpart. As listeners and speakers you stand on absolutely even ground.

There is one aspect of your relationship, however, that is uneven: the focus of interest will always be disproportionate.

When you have chosen to listen to another in a healing way, you carry no expectation that the attention will shift to you. You dedicate yourself to concentrating on the other's words, the other's issues, and the other's life. You place upon center stage the development, the well-being, and the wholeness of the one who has turned to you.

From the time you begin listening until listening's end, you live out the truth that you're equal in every way, save one. The other person will always have it over you as far as focus of attention is concerned.

The only thing that matters is the everlasting present.
W. Somerset Maugham

~

Eternity is not something that begins after you are dead.
It is going on all the time. We are in it now.
Charlotte Perkins Gilman

~

We must not allow the clock and the calendar
to blind us to the fact that each moment of life
is a miracle and a mystery.
H. G. Wells

A healing listener stays in the moment.

The present contains all there is. People of wisdom have taught for millennia: the past is gone; the future may never be; the present holds everything. The practice of healing listening both asks you and helps you to live this truth.

Each time you listen in a healing way, you bring yourself completely into the present moment. Rather than thinking about another time or reliving a previous experience, you focus your attention on *this* experience. Rather than anticipating what you're going to say or do, you give yourself over to the fullness of the moments the two of you share, one after another. In doing so, it is as if time slows, and the present instant opens, and more is there than you expected.

If, as the other is speaking, you're trying to figure out what their past was like or carrying concern for what their future will hold, you will not be free to receive all they bring. This is not to say that yesterdays and tomorrows aren't a valid focus. They certainly can be. But it's up to the other person to direct the focus in the present moment you share.

Bringing yourself into the now, and staying there, takes discipline. Few of us can do this consistently. Most of us need continual reminders. And this is another way healing listening can be a help for daily living. The more you intentionally center yourself in the present with the one who's speaking, the more these moments will be well-sensed, well-used, well-lived.

The saying is true: the way you live your moments is the way you live your life. For a healing listener, that's an inviting prospect.

Next to love, quietness.
English Proverb

And silence, like a poultice, comes
To heal the blows of sound.
Oliver Wendell Holmes

There is no music in a "rest,"
but there is the making of music in it.
John Ruskin

A healing listener consciously stills.

It's difficult to hear what another person has to say with too much noise around. This is obviously true about the sounds that can pollute any environment—blaring radios, insistent telephones, loud traffic, distracting conversations. Your role as listener includes finding ways to reduce certain noises and eliminate others. Truth is, however, that the most bothersome noises and the most disruptive activities do not come from around you as the listener. They come from within you.

When your mind wanders all over the place, it gets in the way of your listening. When a persistent dialogue is going on inside your head, it limits how accurately you can hear what the other is saying. If your eyes are continually looking around, or if you're constantly fidgeting, you're creating another kind of "noise" that will hamper how well you connect with the one before you.

As you become increasingly quiet within and without, you create an atmosphere in which the other person can speak more naturally and be heard more easily. This is more than the passive process of becoming still—it is *making* still. It is stilling used as an active verb: "I still my mind. I calm my body. I quiet my soul."

Irish poet William Butler Yeats once wrote, "We can make our minds so like still water that beings gather about us to see their own images. . . ." Your still presence gives others the opportunity to see their own reflection. Your quiet being offers a hush in which others can find and hear their own voices.

The ear is the road to the heart.
Voltaire

We pine for kindred natures
To mingle with our own.
Felicia Hemans

The more you join in with people
in their joys and their sorrows,
the nearer and dearer they come to be to you.
Samuel Clemens

A healing listener draws close.

It seems self-evident: the closer you sit or stand or walk with another, the better you'll be able to hear. Close proximity facilitates good listening. Yet the act of drawing near is a way for you to speak as well as listen.

By approaching another in an unthreatening way, and allowing or encouraging another to come closer to you, you open a mutual space, a common field, just for the two of you. It's as if you're saying, "This space is now ours and no one else's. We are alone in this togetherness." Your drawing close offers privacy and suggests safety.

A second message you communicate is, "I am not standing back. I am choosing to come toward you in this encounter." Leaning slightly toward the other can be another way of saying, "I am with you. I am ready to hear more."

The most important act of drawing close is an internal one. You move inwardly toward the other person so that you're together not so much shoulder to shoulder but heart to heart and soul to soul. You relate with a posture that remembers and affirms the words of the Roman playwright Terence: "I am a person: I hold that nothing human is alien to me."

If you believe nothing human is alien to you, the other will know it and feel confirmed by you. Then whether you're next to one another in the same room, or many miles are between you as the two of you communicate, still the other will sense you are drawing close.

Separation secures manifest friendship.
Indian Proverb

One is to have part of one's life to oneself.
Samuel Johnson

The field cannot well be seen
from within the field.
Ralph Waldo Emerson

A healing listener keeps a distance.

"You just wrote I'm to draw close," you're thinking. "Now you say I'm not. Make up your mind. Do I get close or do I keep my distance?" The answer is simple: yes and yes.

Yes, you are to come close enough to hear easily and see well. Near enough to show you're open, interested, and willing to listen.

And yes, you are to make sure you keep adequate distance between you. It's important to be sensitive to the other person's physical space and not draw too close for their comfort. In certain cases it's also wise to be friendly without the expectation that you'll be a friend in an ongoing way. Real emotional closeness, while it can be instantaneous, usually generates over time. It's impossible to extend such a relationship to everyone. It's also good to remember that the other person is usually looking not so much for affection as for acceptance.

Your role involves knowing about and maintaining an appropriate and healthy separation between you as two unique individuals. A listening relationship is not the place to deal with your personal issues nor to assume responsibility for the other's issues. Those to whom you listen must be responsible for their own feelings, their own decisions, their own lives.

Keeping a distance between you can bring a sense of security to those who turn to you. Many will find comfort in knowing you are not in the same place emotionally or spiritually that they are. If they're agitated, you're calm. If they're flighty, you're grounded. If they feel lost, you're familiar with the surrounding terrain. By listening from your own separate foundation, you participate in an experience of stability and safety that can open the door to hope.

When people come face to face,
their differences vanish.
Chinese Proverb

The countenance is the portrait of the mind,
the eyes are its informer.
Marcus Cicero

A friend is one before whom I may think aloud.
Ralph Waldo Emerson

A healing listener faces.

When you choose to listen in a healing way, you lead with your face. Sometimes you'll listen as you sit, stand, or perhaps lie opposite the one who's speaking. This is the most direct way of communicating. In certain circumstances it's the most intimate way. But some people may perceive this head-on approach as potentially challenging. So you may wish to shift your position and discover a more comfortable angle that both suits the other person and gives each of you the freedom to look at one another as you please.

Speakers commonly look at their listeners about half the time when they talk one on one. Listeners tend to watch their speakers more, perhaps three-quarters of the time. It's worth remembering that looking at the other without letup can feel disconcerting to them, and even a little threatening.

By physically turning toward the other, you offer yourself at your most expressive. Opening your countenance to someone is the clearest way of saying, "This is the genuine me." In so doing, you invite the genuine in the other to appear. You underline this message by opening yourself in other ways as well—uncrossing your legs and arms, relaxing your shoulders, opening your hands, using your natural voice.

Depending on your relationship, your role, and how the other person prefers to communicate, you may do your listening as you walk or ride side by side, as you work or play shoulder to shoulder. Sometimes you'll need to find ways to turn yourself toward the other as you communicate by telephone or through a computer. You can still face one another without physically doing so.

You can observe a lot just by watching.
Yogi Berra

Don't think; look.
Ludwig Wittgenstein

The face is the mirror of the mind,
and eyes without speaking
confess the secrets of the heart.
Jerome

A healing listener listens with the eyes.

When you listen to what someone is saying, you're likely at times to rely more on your eyes than your ears. Studies show that well over half of the meaning of spoken messages comes from that which can only be seen: how the speaker looks and moves. About a third of the spoken message comes from what the ear can pick up: the tone of voice, the rhythm of the words, and the rate of speaking. Only a small amount of the message comes from the words themselves.

Seeing is instrumental for hearing in this elemental way: lip reading. Whether you're conscious of it or not, you're almost always reading other people's lips as they speak. Your ears depend upon your eyes to help take in what is spoken as well as to confirm what is heard.

Even more important is the role your eyes play in interpreting what others are really saying beneath their words as you pay attention to their faces. With its intricate weave of muscles, the human face can display more than 8,000 expressions, and it can do so in a fraction of a second. And the face can make these displays *for* a mere fraction of a second, almost faster than can be seen. Almost faster, but not quite, for your eyes do catch these nuances and pass them on to be received as information for your brain. Your eyes automatically record the other person's gestures and gait, their poses and postures, and send all those along to be added to the interpretation.

Of course, no part of a speaker's body is more expressive than the eyes. That's one reason why listeners spend so much time looking at those colorful spheres. Herman Melville was right: "The eyes are the gateway to the soul." Many times your eyes can fathom what your ears can only hope to.

For all the talk you hear
about knowledge being such a wonderful thing,
instinct is worth forty of it
for real unerringness.
Samuel Clemens

The eye is the traitor of the heart.
Thomas Wyatt

When the eyes say one thing, and the tongue another,
a practiced person relies on the language of the first.
Ralph Waldo Emerson

A healing listener listens with the third ear.

We have a capacity to hear more than sound, to listen beyond what is spoken. That ability comes from our "third ear." The idea for this third ear started with the philosopher Friedrich Nietzsche and was later adapted by the psychiatrist Theodor Reik. They described an invisible ear that can hear what physical ears cannot.

Have you ever had the sense that you knew what another was feeling even if they did not tell you, or even if they told you the opposite? Something intuitive within you somehow knew. Beyond their words and even beneath their silences, you can sometimes sense the other person whispering their truth to you, whether it's a feeling or a thought. It is your third ear that catches that whisper. This same ear can also hear similar whispers that come from deep within you when you're listening to another in a healing way. Something instinctual within you murmurs, and the murmur is to be trusted.

These gentle whispers are elusive. If you try too hard to hear them, you're likely to miss them. They come ever so subtly—on glances, minute body movements, almost imperceptible vocal intonations. Usually they are heard not as a result of your thinking but only after you have given up thinking.

Listening with your third ear is never an attempt to psychoanalyze someone or to impose your own perceptions on another's unspoken meanings. It is simply your openness to those messages that may not have been spoken but have been nonetheless sent.

The heart never lies.
Dutch Proverb

The heart has its reasons
that reason knows nothing of.
Blaise Pascal

Where the heart lies,
let the brain lie also.
Robert Browning

A healing listener listens with the heart.

When you listen with your two physical ears, you hear what's actu-
ally spoken. When you listen with your third ear, you're attuned to
what may be unspoken or only hinted at. When you listen with your
heart, you concentrate on what the heart knows best and responds to
most naturally. You focus on feelings.

If you wish to communicate with the whole of the other person,
and in a way that encourages their becoming even more whole as a
human being, you'll listen for that which is heartfelt in them. More
than that, you'll listen from that place within you that readily recog-
nizes the language of the heart—the spontaneous, the fervent, the
genuine. Your heart, like all hearts, naturally detects excitement, joy,
and love. It senses sadness and grief, loneliness and depression, anger
and fear. Your heart engages when people talk honestly about their significant relationships, their tumultuous changes, their unexpected
tragedies. Your heart quickens when others struggle to speak of their
deepest sentiments, their fiercest forebodings, their most humbling
self-revelations.

A deep place in the other reaches out toward a deep place in you,
hoping for a connection. Their heart calls to yours, and when you're at
your listening best, your heart responds, "I am here."

Listening with your heart invites you to stay open to another even
if their feelings are much different from yours, even if the expression of
those feelings is stronger than you expect. In doing so, your heart will
lead you to encounters with your own wholeness too. You cannot separate the one from the other.

Never apologize for showing feeling.
When you do so you apologize for truth.
Benjamin Disraeli

❧

The body is a house of many windows:
there we all sit, showing ourselves. . . .
R. L. Stevenson

❧

Why be given a body if you have to keep it
shut up in a case like a rare, rare fiddle?
Katherine Mansfield

A healing listener listens with the whole body.

Many people treat listening as an above-the-neck activity using the ears, the eyes, the face, and, of course, the brain. It's as if the purpose of the body were only to support and transport the head. Listening that is truly healing, however, calls upon your entire physical being as a vehicle for communication.

Have you ever felt such a strong visceral reaction to something you've seen or heard that it came to you in some way through your body? Maybe your heart beat faster, or your stomach churned, or you held your breath without intending to. A similar process can be at work as you attune yourself to other people by listening to them carefully and caringly. You strain to hear them with all of who you are, including your whole body.

How do you go about this? You pay attention to what's happening within you as you spend time with another. You notice any subtle sensations that may develop in your throat, your chest, your stomach. What about those muscles in your neck, your shoulders, your limbs—do they become either more relaxed or more tense as your time with another goes on? Overall, do you feel lighter or heavier? Is there any change in how deeply you're breathing or how often you take breaths? Do you feel unexpectedly tired or sleepy when you're pretty sure you've had enough rest? Your physical reactions can be indications you're picking up something from the other person that goes beyond the words they're using.

By being fully present in your body and attuned to your physical sensations, you can add an additional, irreplaceable dimension to your listening ability.

Whatever our souls are made of,
yours and mine are the same.
Emily Brontë

Body and spirit are twins:
God only knows which is which.
Algernon Charles Swinburne

There is one spectacle grander than the sea;
that is the sky.
There is one spectacle grander than the sky;
that is the interior of the soul.
Victor Hugo

A healing listener listens through the soul.

If you're going to open yourself to others in their entirety, and if you're willing to bring your whole being to this endeavor, then you'll necessarily include your soul in your listening. To do so is to make contact with a critically important aspect of each of us.

A popular definition for soul comes from the Quaker tradition: "that which is of God in every person." Whether every person has a soul or is a soul, everyone has a connection with the divine. We human beings are more than just human. We carry a spark of the eternal, a touch of that which is divine.

As you continue your healing listening, you become aware that beneath all your knowledge and feelings there lie longings, hungers, and awarenesses that go very deep. It is here that your life purpose resides and your most profound sense of meaning dwells. This is the level on which your soul communes with the soul of the other person.

Sometimes the other's soul releases a natural flow of words, making perfect sense. At other times the words come in stops and starts, unable to capture fully the well of truth within. It's not uncommon for the soul to expose itself through dream images, poetic wording, or simply the sound of reverential silence.

How does your soul hear the soul of another? Perhaps by your forming a prayer as you begin, and holding the other in prayer as you continue. By your watching and listening for signs of the divine within that are carried on the other person's words and nestled between the words. By your letting go of needing to be absolutely clear and embracing absolute mystery when it presents itself. How do you best proceed? Listen to your soul. It will tell you.

Take rather than give the tone
of the company you are in.
Lord Chesterfield

As much as possible, be the slave, not the king.
Allow yourself to be struck.
Be the ball, not the bat.
Rumi

The one who, conscious of being strong,
is content to be weak,
shall be the paragon of all humankind.
Lao Tze

A healing listener surrenders.

It's hard to overestimate the importance of one aspect of being a healing listener: you release your own will so you can follow the lead of the other's will as it relates to the communication between you.

You let go of any attempt to control the one who's talking and to shape whatever they're saying. The agenda is theirs, not yours. It is their direction to be followed, their wisdom to be honored, their life to be witnessed, their thoughts and decisions to be given form.

This surrender includes letting go of the need to insert your ego, however subtly, into this experience. Should you wish to be seen in a prescribed way (as a really good listener, for example), a certain amount of your energy will necessarily be channeled into making sure you are perceived like this. Your surrender may also mean holding back on the impulse to share your own experience, even though the other person's story may resonate closely with yours. You surrender any right to claim the space and time together as your own so that it automatically, unquestionably belongs to the other.

Healing listening asks you to stay out of the way so that what is most healing for another has the best possible chance of appearing and then growing. It involves a mutual invitation to trust in the support that holds both of you as you open together to the mystery of life as it flows.

This is a profoundly selfless way to be with another. It is also a profoundly meaningful way to offer the gift of yourself that comes from beyond yourself.

'Tis a task indeed to learn to hear.
Edward Young

If speaking is silver, listening is gold.
Turkish Proverb

To listen well is a second inheritance.
Publilius Syrus

Healing listeners listen single-mindedly... except when they don't.

"She listened to me as if nothing else mattered at that moment."

"He paid such attention to me, I felt I was the most important person in the world."

Listeners who evoke such comments seem engrossed in the one who is speaking. Supremely attentive, they let little or nothing get in the way of communication.

As a listener, such focused attention is a gift you have to offer. It is not a privilege earned by another but a blessing you freely bestow. Such single-minded interest has the potential to dispel loneliness and instill courage. It can help build esteem and strengthen resolve. It has even been known to save lives, quite literally.

It's worth remembering that this kind of attention takes energy, and from time to time that energy wanes, no matter how much of it you begin with. Studies show that it's difficult for any listener to stay completely focused more than twenty or twenty-five minutes running. When your mind wanders (not *if* but *when*), take a breath, physically shift yourself, and start devoting your attention anew. Be forgiving of yourself when you drift away. Just note what's happening and good-naturedly bring yourself back to the moment. As you do so, you can treat your all-too-human digression as another opportunity for you to become an interested listener all over again.

Never miss a good chance to shut up.
Will Rogers

Speech sows, silence reaps.
Persian Proverb

What shall I say to you?
What can I say
Better than silence is?
Henry Wadsworth Longfellow

A healing listener cleaves to silence.

When people engage in polite conversation, spells of silence usually seem awkward. Longer periods of quiet can feel particularly uncomfortable. Many feel obliged to fill that empty space with words, believing it's the kind and responsible thing to do.

Healing listening is far from polite conversation. In this case, allowing silence and protecting it, rather than escaping it, is what's appropriate and responsible. Being in silence with another may require some practice, because it's the opposite of what's normally expected.

Your listening silence gives the other person's words the stage they deserve. It offers a sense of freedom and expansiveness to the one who wishes to speak. It helps you hear their words more accurately and easily. Your thoughtful quietness can also help the speaker hear herself or himself more clearly.

Such silence is much more than a backdrop. It reaches toward the speaker and asks, "Do you have more to say? Please go ahead." A welcoming quietness issues an invitation: "Do you wish to go deeper? I will go with you." This easygoing stillness gives permission to the other person: "You can say whatever you want and it will be accepted, just as you will be."

Silence that sits comfortably with the two of you has a life of its own. It can be the bearer of truth and wisdom without a word being spoken. Silence like this conveys a sense of peace and acceptance that lies beyond the scope of mere language.

A secret of healing listening is to unite your silence with your attention and your caring. When you do so, the other person will appreciate it, and each part will deepen the others—the silence, the attention, and the caring.

First learn the meaning of what you say,
and then speak.
Epictetus

~

Straight talk ornaments anyone's face.
Spanish Proverb

~

Use what language you will,
you can never say anything but what you are.
Ralph Waldo Emerson

A healing listener speaks.

If it is anything, healing listening is interactive. More than passively accepting what someone says, you actively engage the other person with your comfortable gaze, your attentive silence, and your responsive facial expressions. Yet contradictory as it may seem, being a healing listener requires you to speak.

The other person usually wants to know who you are. Do you speak their language? Are you approachable? Are you as human as they? Are you really interested? Are you trustworthy? If other people are going to open to you at any depth, they want to hear as well as see you.

You don't need to speak much. In fact, you shouldn't. Yet inasmuch as true listening involves understanding as well as possible what's been spoken, the only way to confirm your understanding is to clarify it with the other. Then your speaking becomes an invaluable part of your listening.

You can also speak your listening with short words that show you're with the other: "I see." "Uh huh." "Tell me more." You can paraphrase what's been said, using your own wording, as a way of confirming the other's message. You can reflect what the other has spoken to underline its significance. You can verify what has been communicated by asking a question or two. You can draw out the other with an open-ended comment: "I sense you have something more to say about this."

Your well-spoken, well-timed words need not interrupt the flow of your listening and of the other's speaking. They can encourage and deepen both.

One understands in others
only those feelings
one is capable of producing oneself.
Andre Gide

There are moments when silence,
prolong'd and unbroken,
More expressive may be than all the words ever spoken.
It is when the heart has an instinct of what
In the heart of another is passing.
Owen Meredith

A healing listener "feels into."

Feelings will often be involved as you choose to listen to another in a healing way. If a feeling is spoken about, yours is the opportunity and responsibility to know something of what it's like to have such a feeling. It's not enough to know this by thinking about it. Rather, you "feel into" it. This is the literal meaning of the word *empathy*, which is a foundation for healing listening.

Empathy and sympathy are different. When you sympathize, you attend to the other person's difficult or uncomfortable situation as well as to your own feelings about this person and what is happening to them. For example, you might feel sad that the other person feels sad. When you empathize, you attend only to the other's feelings, not yours. You want to know how it feels to be this other person at that moment. What is going on inside them? How does the world appear through their eyes? What is it like to walk in their shoes?

You invite yourself to move inside that other person temporarily, keeping your senses wide open. Is your intention to change them? No. To improve their situation? Not at all. You simply want to know as fully as you can, with every part of you, the truth of this other person's present lived experience. Then, knowing this, you strive to become more at home with their truth, even if it's not your truth. Especially if it's not your truth.

When you can be at home with another's feelings and honor their right to be who they are and to believe what they believe, you can be an instrument of their movement toward their own healing. This movement is not your doing, yet you're a part of it. And your part becomes a privilege.

The wise adapt themselves to circumstances,
as water molds itself to the pitcher.
Chinese Proverb

Treat a thousand dispositions in a thousand ways.
Ovid

Prepare yourself for the world,
as the athletes used to do for their exercise;
oil your mind and your manners,
to give them the necessary suppleness and flexibility;
strength alone will not do.
Earl of Chesterfield

A healing listener adapts.

"Never interrupt."

"Always face the other person."

"Refrain from offering a tissue to someone who's crying—let them reach for it on their own."

A listening style that abides only by such hard-and-fast rules can eventually get in the way of what's ultimately healing. Healing listening bears in mind who the other is and what is happening to them. It takes into account where and when you encounter one another, as well as what else is going on around you. Then it bends and yields as needed. It adapts.

Being a sensitive listener means adapting to whoever is speaking to you. If there is a choice, where does the other person wish to be in relation to you? How loudly or softly do they wish to speak? How directly do they want to talk about their feelings? What sort of language seems natural and appropriate? Are they comfortable when you offer them what seems to you the right amount of silence? If not, then what?

Your purpose includes adapting to the place where the two of you are talking, whether or not it's as private, quiet, or cozy as you would prefer. Yours is also to accommodate, if necessary, to the time that you share, making the most of how much you each have available. Adapting may mean listening while either of you is engaged in another task at the same time. It may mean listening even if intrusions abound.

Your willingness to be flexible gives a clear signal that you care about the other's needs and desires. It also gives them subtle permission to loosen any rigidity that might unnaturally restrict their freedom when they're with you. Then as you relax and adapt, they can relax and open.

Mark the end.
John Florio

End good, all good.
German Proverb

Listen and attend with the ear of your heart.
Saint Benedict

A healing listener acknowledges the ending of the time together.

"This time ahead is spoken for." That's what you communicate when you begin to listen in a healing way. Whether you say this verbally or nonverbally, it's understood that whatever time you have together is set aside. But eventually this time will come to an end. The timing of this ending may be made clear by what you both agree to in advance. A specified period like this clarifies your availability. It can also help the other person organize and prioritize what they have to say.

Sometimes you will meet without knowing when you'll conclude. If the one you are with is in crisis, for instance, you'll want to be sensitive in determining when it's right to move toward concluding this talk. Or the tone of what's being shared may gradually shift and you're unexpectedly in the midst of something deep, something that asks for a little more time together. However and whenever you bring this time to an end, it helps to name what you're doing and to offer three messages: "yes," "thank you," and "goodbye."

When you say "yes," you affirm the other person and what has just happened: "My, you have shared a lot." "Yes, you are handling this all right." "I believe you are finding your way."

When you say "thank you," you express appreciation for whatever is true: "Thank you for being so open and trusting me." "This was a meaningful talk for me."

By saying a clear "goodbye," you acknowledge that your time of healing listening has been completed. And whether your goodbye means "until next time" or "never again," the two of you move on, each carrying a little of the other as you go.

The strongest principle of growth
lies in the human choice.
Mary Ann Evans

The sense of dignity grows
with the ability to say no.
Abraham Joshua Heschel

Spend time every day listening
to what your muse is trying to tell you.
Saint Bartholomew

Sometimes a healing listener refrains from listening.

Done without any letup, healing listening will deplete you. Even with regular breaks, such listening may tax you more than you expect. Sometimes your energy and ability to focus will fade, if not leave you altogether.

When this occurs, your healthiest response might be to choose to do something else for a while, as a way of refreshing yourself. Then you can come back to listening with renewed capacity. Any breaks you give yourself may be measured in minutes or hours, perhaps days or weeks, or even longer periods.

Alternatively, you may decide it would be best for you if you chose not to be a listener in specific circumstances or with particular people. For example, it makes sense for someone in deep grief to postpone being a healing listener, especially with others who are grieving, until life feels a little more normal again.

One of the most valid reasons for choosing not to listen is simply this: you don't want to. Other ways of spending your limited time on earth may invite you. You may decide to explore a book, a museum, or a landscape. You may engage in a hobby, a sport, or some exciting adventure. You may give yourself over to the very valid occupation of lying idle for a while, knowing how replenishing that can be. The philosopher Bertrand Russell was right: "The time you enjoy wasting is not wasted time."

In addition, there are lots of meaningful and enjoyable ways to spend time with people other than your being a healing listener. So why limit yourself? Life is too short for that.

An ounce of patience
is worth a pound of brains.
Dutch Proverb

Patience is the greatest prayer.
Hindu Proverb

Be plastered with patience.
William Langland

Healing listening requires a triple dose of patience.

All of us have a lesson to learn about patience—not once but over the whole course of our lives. Not surprisingly, the invitation to learn patience will be everywhere you turn as a healing listener.

First, there is the process itself. Who knows how long healing takes? Shakespeare was right: "What wound did ever heal but by degrees?" Who knows how much listening is needed before it is enough? Only the patient find out.

You dare not hurry healing listening itself. Should you attempt to do so, it will become less healing. The one who's speaking will then not open up naturally and comfortably. They may not touch upon all that is important, and something critical will remain missing. Human growth often requires periods in which change is allowed to unfold as it will, which means that temporarily it may not unfold at all. This all takes time, which takes patience.

You'll be asked to be patient with the other person. Each one to whom you listen will be unique and set in their own ways. One may use many more words than you wish. Another may circle a subject before finally moving in. Others may repeat themselves, intentionally or unintentionally, as they search for what's true. There is a universal fact to be aware of and remember: listeners can process verbal information three times as fast as their counterparts normally talk. Time after time you'll need to slow down and be patient in your listening.

Morever, patience is required for what you bring to this experience too. Sometimes you'll miss or forget important information. You may not give others the silence they need. You may say something unhelpful or unthoughtful. As a healing listener you'll need to practice patience with yourself as you reach the potential that healing has to offer.

Humility is attentive patience.
Simone Weil

❧

The four cardinal virtues are
humility, humility, humility,
and humility.
Bernard of Clairveaux

❧

I long to accomplish a great and noble task,
but it is my chief duty to accomplish humble tasks
as though they were great and noble.
Helen Keller

Healing listening rests on humility.

When you approach others with your authentic self, you come before them less than perfect. If you're being genuine, you will not be able to hide your fallibilities and shortcomings. That's humbling. This is not the only way healing listening rests on humility.

Many times you will listen well, and this will be satisfying for each of you, for both of you. At other times, no matter how much you intend and wish otherwise, you'll not be as present as you could be. This is humbling too, because you would like your listening to consistently offer its full potential. Humbling also is the realization that there is so much you don't know, and cannot know, about this whole experience.

There will be times when you will be entrusted with feelings that go very deep and with revelations that are poignantly touching. The other person may speak words to you they have never spoken to another human being. It is humbling to be invited to be a part of people's lives in this way.

Healing listening is by its very nature a regular practice in humility. Since it involves your not doing more than your doing, this listening is about something other than personal accomplishment. Nor is it something for which you can take credit. You are a channel for any healing, not its source. Your listening is the occasion for any growth, not its cause.

Finally, it is clear that your listening is far more than just yours. You join a stream of intuitive wisdom as you add to it your own wisdom. There is a real sense in which healing listening is a gift you receive more than an offering you make. For that reason, it is an occasion for heartfelt humility and gratitude.

Trust thyself: every heart vibrates to that iron string.
Ralph Waldo Emerson

Wisdom is oft times nearer when we stoop
Than when we soar.
William Wordsworth

Every man is more than just himself;
he also represents the unique, the very special
and always significant and remarkable point
at which the world's phenomena intersect,
only once in this way and never again.
Hermann Hesse

Healing listeners trust they are enough.

You will not always feel ready when you're called upon to be a listener. You may be thrust into situations with no time to anticipate or prepare. You may be exposed to issues that seem terribly complex or feelings that seem unusually complicated. You may wonder if your wisdom or experience is adequate for what the other person is revealing to you. Should that happen, say this to yourself: "I am enough."

There is a reason this person has turned to you. They must see something in you or sense something coming from you that leads them to choose to be with you. If they can trust in your potential as a healing listener, can you not trust it too?

You can also trust that whatever has happened in your life so far has helped you prepare for this particular encounter. Your past successes have given you confidence. Your past difficulties have added to your repertoire of experience. Your past failures have taught you valuable lessons. All that you have been through is another reason to believe you are enough.

There is something more you can trust: your authenticity. When you are your most genuine self, others sense it, value it, and respond positively. Your unaffected naturalness can be another way of assuring that you are enough.

You can be more at ease as a healing listener when you realize you are not alone. Anyone who has influenced or taught you as a listener is with you. Everyone in the growing cadre of healing listeners joins with you in spirit, and sometimes their presence can feel quite palpable. And, of course, the true Source of all healing is always there too, and that presence can be the most palpable of all.

Such ever was love's way:

to rise, it stoops.

Robert Browning

It is the heart always that sees,
before the head can see.

Thomas Carlyle

Listen with your mind
in your heart.

Theophan the Recluse

Healing listening is, at basis, an act of love.

At the center of all healing listening lies this principle: you strive to listen to another person as you would wish to be listened to yourself.

If your life were in upheaval and you turned to someone to be with you during this time, you would want them to listen without interrupting your words, without diverting your train of thought, without stifling your expression of feelings. You would want them to accept what you had to say without disapproval or pulling back. You would want them to stay with you for an appropriate length of time. That would be a loving response on their part.

If you were overcome with deep and perhaps conflicting emotions and wanted to share these with someone, you would appreciate the effort they made to understand what it was like to be in your place. You would find comfort in their calmness, security in their stillness, and validation in their patience. If words left you, you would find it meaningful if they could sit with you in the silence. In doing so, you would feel they were still in dialogue with you, their heart nestling your heart, their soul touching your soul.

If you were struggling for insight or meaning or hope for your life, you would find it helpful if this other person did not rush in with ready solutions or easy answers. They would give your thoughts and feelings the weight they deserved by accepting these quietly and reflectively. You would find it gratifying that they paid close enough attention that they remembered what you had said, and helped you remember it too.

If you wondered what the future held for you, or how you could possibly make it through the present moment, you would find it meaningful if your listener believed the way ahead could eventually open, even if you did not believe it. There would be something about their trust that would encourage your trust. There would be something about their belief in life and their faith in matters larger than life that could inspire your own belief and faith, if not today, then tomorrow.

You would feel grateful that someone had put their personal interests aside long enough to give you their full presence and focus. As they listened, you would clearly sense that they valued you, respected you, even enjoyed you. You would feel blessed and reassured that they willingly offered their gifts to you: not just their time and energy, but their openness, their genuineness, their humanness. In a word, you would know they had offered you nothing less than their love. And you would feel grateful.

Such is the lasting effect of healing listening.

Afterword

It's a summer Sunday afternoon as I finish writing this book. A friend has just left our home. I'll call her Ann.

Ann's days are in disarray. A grown son is in serious legal trouble—again. His addictions compound the problem. His career plans have been dashed. To make matters even worse, he has an illness that threatens his life. Normal family life is a thing of the past. She feels frazzled, incredibly sad, painfully angry.

Plans called for Ann to meet us at our house, and then go to lunch at a nearby restaurant. My wife Bernie and I thought about the Sunday noon crowds, the lack of privacy at the tables, the impersonality of that public space, and decided to cook a simple brunch for her instead: an egg dish, her favorite grilled vegetables, fresh fruit, muffins. When Ann arrived, she seemed pleased at the change in plans.

Cups of coffee in hand, Bernie and I sat with Ann on our screened porch, overlooking the small lake. A midday breeze and the songs of birds were the only surrounding sounds. Ann immediately began spilling out the trying events of her recent days. Her feelings rotated from sadness to anger to fear and back again. We moved inside and she talked through much of the meal. Afterward Bernie and Ann retreated to the porch while I did the cleanup. They talked more about what was happening to Ann, but they talked also about other things they shared in common as a result of almost four decades of friendship.

I stood at the kitchen sink and had three thoughts.

"What a healing listener Bernie is!" I thought. "I write about healing listening and she embodies it. I'm the one who's trained, yet she brings it to life every bit as well as I, if not better." Does that fact say anything to you who read these words?

My second thought: Even though I knew intellectually I could not solve Ann's problems for her, there was still a tiny part of me, after all these years of experience, that was tempted to try. "Maybe I could talk some sense into her son," I said to myself before quickly dismissing the thought, feeling a little embarrassed that I had even momentarily entertained it. Does that impulse of mine say anything to you who read these words?

This was my third thought as I heard their muffled voices around the corner: There was a small sense in which I continued to be a healing listener as I provided space for the two of them to keep talking, woman to woman, and as I breathed a short prayer that healing energy would surround them. Does that sense of mine confirm anything in your experience?

Ann left two and a half hours after she came. She gave us long hugs at the door. Tears came to her eyes as she said, "You don't know how much this has helped me! What you have done was truly life-giving to me today."

What had Bernie and I done? Problem-solved? No. Offered to intervene with her son? Thankfully not. Assured her that she would feel better tomorrow? We couldn't. We don't know what tomorrow will hold for her or her family.

We listened. We accepted whatever she had to say. We believed in her integrity as a wife, a mother, a human being. We held on to the certainty that she has possessed reservoirs of strength and courage in the past, and that she can tap into them again. We held the hope that she will find ways to live with the uncertainty of life she is experiencing.

We listened to her, and stayed with her, and believed that healing can come. That is all. And we learned once again that it is everything.

Acknowledgements

One more time I am keenly aware that it takes a village to write a book.

John Peterson was the first person who said, after reading an early draft, "Yes, Jim, this has the makings of something to be shared." Then he regularly made himself available to offer feedback over the course of the following months, as he has done for so many of my projects since we were introduced to one another fifteen years ago. Jennifer Levine returned as a reader and advisor, bringing her knowledge of psychology, her familiarity with spirituality, and her dependable and loving frankness. Charles Klingler graciously offered his masterful way with words and grammar several times through the months of writing, but especially at the very end.

The Willowgreen family came to the rescue, as always. Clare Barton and Sue Devito came up with words when I could not, edited copy, and looked over my shoulder as the book headed toward print. They also kept the office functioning smoothly when I blithely disappeared for extended periods to research, write, and photograph.

My personal family turned up in greater numbers than usual. My wife Bernie was predictably sensitive, responsive, and helpful from beginning to end. Sometimes it's no fun being married to a man who always has a new project going. My daughter Christen Pettit Miller added her wisdom as a pastoral minister and naturally gifted writer. Her husband Robert Pettit added his insights as an editor, professor, and all-around scholar.

The two people who were so critically important to the writing of *The Art of Being a Healing Presence* two years ago repeated their roles. Susan Cutshall offered advice, feedback, moral support, and her patented candlelightings at just the right moment time after time. Jinnie Draper repeatedly said, "Jim, you know this better than I," then would say or write something that was far beyond my ability to say it or write it. Both Susan and Jinnie did their utmost to keep me honest.

Very early in the research Andrew Colvin generously shared the ideas he and Carolyn Gwynn Coakley had developed about the various kinds of listening, as found in their book *Perspectives on Listening* (Ablex, 1993).

This project was the first occasion I've had to with work Peggy Gerardot as a graphic designer and artist. I quickly marveled at her creativity and enthusiasm and appreciated the dedication she brought to this book.

I am deeply grateful to have known such kind and generous support throughout this project. I am blessed to be part of such a caring village.

VIDEOTAPES BY JAMES E. MILLER

Invincible Summer
Listen to Your Sadness
How Do I Go On?
Nothing Is Permanent Except Change
By the Waters of Babylon
We Will Remember
Gaining a Heart of Wisdom
Awaken to Hope
Be at Peace
The Natural Way of Prayer
You Shall Not Be Overcome
The Grit and Grace of Being a Caregiver
Why Yellow?
Common Bushes Afire
When Mourning Dawns
All Seasons Shall Be Sweet
My Shepherd Is the Lord
Still Waters
The Art of Listening in a Healing Way

BOOKS BY JAMES E. MILLER

Welcoming Change

Autumn Wisdom

The Caregiver's Book

When You Know You're Dying

One You Love Is Dying

When You're Ill or Incapacitated/When You're the Caregiver

What Will Help Me?/How Can I Help?

How Will I Get Through the Holidays?

Winter Grief, Summer Grace

A Pilgrimage Through Grief

Helping the Bereaved Celebrate the Holidays

Effective Support Groups

The Rewarding Practice of Journal Writing

One You Love Has Died

When Mourning Dawns

Finding Hope

The Art of Being a Healing Presence

My Shepherd Is the Lord

The Art of Listening in a Healing Way

James E. Miller is a writer/photographer, spiritual director, and grief counselor who lectures and presents in the areas of healing presence, caregiving, spirituality, loss and grief, and managing transition. He founded Willowgreen Productions, Willowgreen Publishing, and Willowgreen Consulting after two decades in the United Methodist ministry.

Jim leads multiple-day workshops on "The Art of Being a Healing Presence" for both professional and lay caregivers in retreat-type settings. He also conducts one-, two- and three-day workshops on being a healing presence as well as other topics for organizations and institutions at the location of their choice. For additional information contact:

10351 Dawson's Creek Boulevard, Suite B
Fort Wayne, Indiana 46825
260/490-2222
jmiller@willowgreen.com . www.willowgreen.com